CAMBRIDGE INTRODUCTION TO THE HISTORY OF MANKIND · TOPIC BOOK
GENERAL EDITOR · TREVOR CAIRNS

Sir Henry Unton Elizabethan Gentleman

Angela Cox

CAMBRIDGE UNIVERSITY PRESS
Cambridge
London   New York   New Rochelle
Melbourne   Sydney

Published by the Press Syndicate of the University of Cambridge
The Pitt Building, Trumpington Street, Cambridge CB2 1RP
32 East 57th Street, New York, NY 10022, USA
296 Beaconsfield Parade, Middle Park, Melbourne 3206, Australia

First published 1982

Printed in Great Britain by
Fakenham Press Limited, Fakenham, Norfolk

British Library cataloguing in publication data
Cox, Angela, 1945–
    Sir Henry Unton, Elizabethan gentleman. –
    (Cambridge introduction to the history of mankind)
    1. Unton, Sir Henry, c. 1557–1596
    2. Ambassadors – England – Biography
    3. Soldiers – England – Biography
    I. Title
    942.05′5′0924   DA35.8.U5   80–42000

ISBN 0 521 22549 3

The author is most grateful to Dr Roy Strong for permission to draw upon his article 'Sir Henry Unton and his Portrait: An Elizabethan Memorial Picture and its History', *Archaeologia*, XCIX (1965), 53–76.

The other major written source for information on the Unton family is *The Unton Inventories*, ed. J. G. Nichols, Berkshire Ashmolean Society, 1841.

All the pictures reproduced in this book date from Elizabethan times. The woodcuts on pages 10, 16, 20 (top) were illustrations to political and social ballads which were collected and published as *The Roxburgh Ballads* in 1847.

The picture on page 20 (bottom) is from Raphael Holinshed, *A Chronicle of England, Scotland and Ireland*, published in London in 1577 and dedicated to William Cecil, Baron Burghley.

The picture on page 21 is from R. Glover, *Nobilitas politica vel curtis*, London 1608.

The picture of Oriel college on page 11 was drawn by John Bereblock. It is from *Collegiorum scholarumque publicarum Academiae Oxoniensis* by Thomas Neale presented to the Bodleian Library by John More in 1630. These are the earliest drawings of Oxford buildings and may have been presented to Queen Elizabeth when she visited Oxford in September 1566.

The author and publisher thank the following for permission to reproduce other illustrations: pages 4–5 and details of the memorial picture throughout, 15, 24, 27 National Portrait Gallery, London; page 10 courtesy of the Marquess of Bath, Longleat House; page 13 courtesy of Mr Simon Wingfield Digby, Sherborne Castle; page 14 Bodleian Library, Oxford.

Map by Reg Piggott.

cover: *Details from a memorial picture of Sir Henry Unton 1557?–96, painted by an unknown artist about 1596, and now in the National Portrait Gallery, London.*

Sir Henry, Lady Dorothy and guests watch a masque after a banquet (front), and Sir Henry ill in bed, attended by doctor, friends and servants (back).

Contents

Introduction

Towards the end of the reign of Queen Elizabeth I, a rich widow decided to have a picture made of the life of her husband, Sir Henry Unton, who had recently died in France. The widow, Lady Dorothy Unton, gave careful instructions about the most important events to the painter, and he included them all in one picture. Although Sir Henry Unton is not famous like Lord Burghley or Sir Francis Drake, he was an important man in his day. His picture life-story is the only one of its kind, and it tells us a great deal about what life was like for the nobility and gentry who ruled Elizabethan England.

When historians set about discovering the past, they look for anything which has survived from the time they are investigating. Such things are called 'original sources'. They may be buildings, furniture, clothes, weapons, letters and documents of all sorts, or pictures. The memorial picture of Sir Henry Unton is just such an original source. Your diary or your photograph album, if it survived into the twenty-first century, could become an original source for an historian studying the present time.

Sir Henry Unton lived an eventful and interesting life. By examining each little picture within the main picture and by using other original sources to extend our knowledge still further, we shall try to discover what it may have been like to be a well-born man in England about four hundred years ago.

The portrait of Sir Henry himself looms large in the centre of the picture. He is shown writing, possibly a letter to the Queen, for he was twice her ambassador in France. The skeleton holding the hour glass indicates that Sir Henry was already dead when the portrait was painted and is a grim reminder to all who look on the picture, that death spares no one. The Elizabethans were more frank and less tactful about death than we are.

The picture reads from right to left. In the top right-hand corner the sun shines on the life of Sir Henry Unton, while on the left the moon illuminates his death.

1 Childhood

Henry Unton as a baby is held by his mother, shown seated beneath a large coat of arms. The coronet on top indicates that she is a countess.

As we might expect, the life-story picture begins with childhood. In the bottom right-hand corner, we enter a house through the porch and discover a scene with a mother cradling her baby. A nurse holds out her arms to receive the child and will perhaps place him in the wickerwork cradle at his mother's side. The baby is wrapped in red velvet, but underneath he is bound tightly in strips of linen. These swaddling bands not only helped to keep the baby warm, they were intended to restrict the movement of its limbs altogether. People used to believe that this was necessary to make sure babies' arms and legs grew straight and strong. It also kept them calm and docile. The two ladies on the left-hand side are probably relatives or friends (not servants, because one of them holds a fan made of feathers), who have come to see the baby.

The room in the picture is simply furnished, though the individual items are costly. The mother is sitting on a comfortable upholstered chair, perhaps the 'chair of wrought crimson velvet' placed on 'one red carpet of cloth, fringed with red and yellow', which we know belonged to the family. The rest of the floor is covered with woven straw matting, that only the rich could afford. The stools are probably of oak wood and black leather. The table at the back is laid with a linen cloth and assorted flagons, tankards and bowls made of silver plate. Everyone shown in the room wears costume of the 1590s (characterized by the enormous ruff), not the costume of the late 1550s, when Henry was a baby.

You may have noticed that the mother and baby are proportionately much larger than the other people in the room. This is to show that they are the most important people there. Above the mother's head is a coat of arms with a coronet. The white strip of letters, now no longer easily readable, tells who the mother and baby are.

'This worthy and famous gentleman, Sir Henry Unton, was son unto Sir Edward Unton, Knight . . . and also his mother, the most virtuous Lady Anne Seymour, countess of Warwick, eldest daughter to the Lord Edward Seymour, duke of Somerset, uncle to King Edward and so protector of his person, and the realm. Her uncles were Thomas and Henry Seymour, which Thomas was Lord Admiral of England and married unto Catherine Parr, last wife of King Henry VIII. Her mother was duchess of Somerset; her aunt was the Lady Jane Seymour, queen of England.'

Sir Henry's mother, the Lady Anne Seymour, had a tragic life. Because she was a first cousin of young King Edward VI, and was so well connected with other leading figures at Court, she became an unwilling victim of a political plot. Her father, the Duke of Somerset, arranged her marriage to John Dudley, Earl of Warwick, the son of his rival the Duke of Northumberland. This marriage, which took place in June 1549, was intended to patch up the quarrel between the two dukes. Nonetheless, the ambitious Duke of Northumberland plotted to bring about Somerset's downfall eighteen months later, and had him executed for treason in January 1552.

In 1553, King Edward VI was dying. Northumberland persuaded Edward to make a will naming Lady Jane Grey as Queen in place of Edward's half-sister the Catholic Princess Mary. Lady Jane was married to another of Northumberland's sons, Lord Guildford Dudley. Lady Jane Grey was Queen for only nine days. Princess Mary swiftly assembled an army to support her rightful claim to the throne. The Duke of Northumberland, the innocent Lady Jane, her husband and his three brothers, including the Earl of Warwick, were imprisoned in the Tower of London. Northumberland was beheaded in August 1553 and his sons, the four Dudley brothers, remained in the Tower until 18 October 1554. John, Earl of Warwick died ten days after his release.

All this may seem very complicated, but it is important to understand the upheavals at court in the mid-sixteenth century. It is important also because Sir Henry was able to take advantage of his powerful relatives for the advancement of his own career.

Six months after Warwick's death, the widowed Countess Anne married again. Her second husband was a country gentleman, Sir Edward Unton of Faringdon and their marriage was celebrated at Hatford church in Berkshire. Sir Edward was so far beneath her in rank (which mattered very much in those days) that the marriage can only be explained as a desperate move by Anne to remove herself from the notice of Queen Mary and to avoid further harm by severing her connections with the court. Sir Edward Unton had land in north Berkshire and Oxfordshire. The countess bore him five sons and two daughters. It is not known exactly when Henry was born at Ascott-under-Wychwood in Oxfordshire, but it was probably in 1557. Three sons died young, but the other four children, Edward, Henry, Cecily and Anne, survived into adulthood. From 1566, the countess is known to have suffered fits of madness, possibly the result of her earlier sufferings. She died in 1588.

On the whole, childhood was a harsh experience at this time and many babies died in infancy. For this reason babies were always baptised immediately after birth.

Rich children like Henry and his brother and sisters were cared for by a nurse until they went to school or had a tutor. They seldom saw their parents. Most children were beaten if they were naughty, often for very slight offences. 'Spare the rod and spoil the child' was a widespread belief in those days.

King Henry VIII and his wives

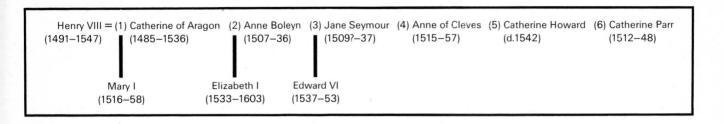

Henry VIII = (1) Catherine of Aragon (2) Anne Boleyn (3) Jane Seymour (4) Anne of Cleves (5) Catherine Howard (6) Catherine Parr
(1491–1547)   (1485–1536)   (1507–36)   (1509?–37)   (1515–57)   (d.1542)   (1512–48)

Mary I   Elizabeth I   Edward VI
(1516–58)   (1533–1603)   (1537–53)

Sir Henry Unton's family tree
*showing his relationship to the
Seymours and Dudleys.*

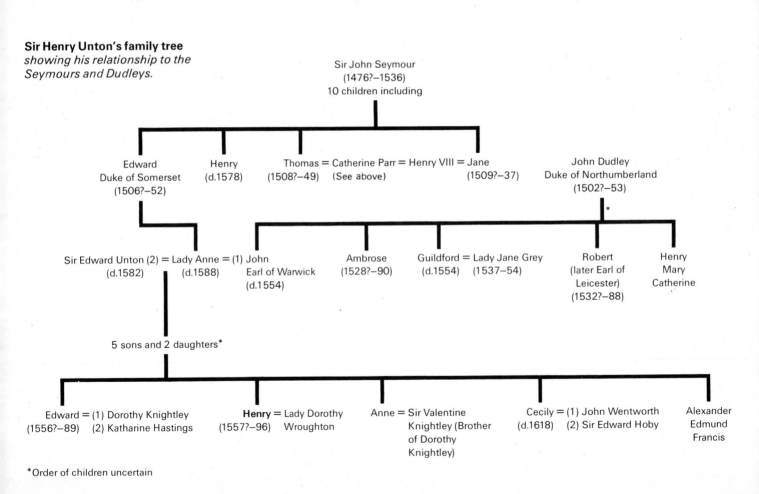

Sir John Seymour
(1476?–1536)
10 children including

Edward   Henry   Thomas = Catherine Parr = Henry VIII = Jane   John Dudley
Duke of Somerset   (d.1578)   (1508?–49) (See above)   (1509?–37)   Duke of Northumberland
(1506?–52)   (1502?–53)

Sir Edward Unton (2) = Lady Anne = (1) John   Ambrose   Guildford = Lady Jane Grey   Robert   Henry
(d.1582)   (d.1588)   Earl of Warwick   (1528?–90)   (d.1554)   (1537–54)   (later Earl of Mary
                                   (d.1554)   Leicester)   Catherine
                                                                                                      (1532?–88)

5 sons and 2 daughters*

Edward = (1) Dorothy Knightley   **Henry** = Lady Dorothy   Anne = Sir Valentine   Cecily = (1) John Wentworth   Alexander
(1556?–89) (2) Katharine Hastings   (1557?–96) Wroughton   Knightley (Brother   (d.1618) (2) Sir Edward Hoby   Edmund
                                                                         of Dorothy   Francis
                                                                         Knightley)

*Order of children uncertain

Very little has been written about early childhood by people who lived in the sixteenth century. We get some clues from portraits, at least of the wealthy. Their toys were usually made of wood and included hoops, rattles, spinning tops and dolls. They also played with cards, chess, solitaire and similar board games. Boys as young as five would start learning to shoot with bow and arrow, to ride and hunt. At a similarly early age girls would start to sew and embroider. Both sexes learnt to dance and play musical instruments.

We notice, too, in the portraits that children over the age of four or five are wearing costume exactly like their parents. This shows that they were expected to behave themselves with adult manners from a very early age.

Lord Cobham with his wife Frances Newton (left), her sister Jane and the Cobham's six children, painted in 1567. The ages of the children are painted above their heads (from the left), 2, 1, 6, twins of 5, 4. People had large families in the sixteenth century but many babies died and many women died in childbirth including a Queen, Jane Seymour.

The children are wearing their best clothes with fashionable ruffs, padded sleeves and jewels like those of the adults.

Notice the birds and animals and the bird-perch on the table. The table is richly set for dessert with grapes, cherries, peaches, apples, pears and nuts. The plates are silver and the wine goblet is gold.

Portraits of whole families were unusual in sixteenth-century England. This one is probably by the artist known as the master of the Countess of Warwick.

9

2 Education and travels

When Henry was about six or seven he began his formal education either at home with a private tutor, or at school, we do not know which. Wherever he was educated, the schooling was strict and monotonous. The main subject was Latin and it is probable that he had to speak Latin all the time he was in school. There were several reasons for this. In the past all education had been given by priests and all books and documents were therefore written in Latin, the language of the Church. Moreover, Latin was the language always used in the law. Since the Renaissance, educated people had become interested once more in classical Roman culture, and that

A contemporary woodcut of a schoolmaster dictating to his pupils. The master wears a scholar's black gown and sits in a big chair at the top of the table. The artist has shown him much bigger than the pupils to emphasise his importance. The pupils, all boys, seem to be writing, possibly on slates because paper would have been expensive. Books were very expensive too. There are only a few in this classroom and they are on high shelves.

meant more Latin still. Henry studied Latin literature in order to imitate the style of the most admired ancient Roman writers, Cicero, Virgil and Ovid. He may have learnt a little Greek and he certainly studied religion. As the son of a well-educated countess, he probably also learnt what were called 'modern subjects', suitable for a gentleman destined to take up public duties. These subjects were history, geography, mathematics and modern languages.

His day at school or at home started early. He would be awake by 5.30 and begin his studies soon afterwards. At school there were lessons in the morning until 11 a.m. with a short break at 9 a.m. The afternoon began at 1 p.m. and continued until 5 or 5.30 p.m., with a break in the middle. At school, as at home, children were severely flogged for acts of disobedience or for neglecting their studies. No wonder Shakespeare describes the 'whining schoolboy with his satchel ... creeping like snail unwillingly to school'. The satchel contained an ink-horn, paper, quill pen and knife to sharpen the nib. Books were scarce and children were expected to learn long passages in them by heart. However not everyone believed that discipline should be so severe. Roger Ascham, Queen Elizabeth's tutor and the author of an influential book, *The Schoolmaster*, believed such harsh treatment did harm rather than good. Boys, he wrote, 'carry commonly from the school with them a hatred of their master and a continual contempt for learning'.

The next part of Henry's education is recorded in the picture. He appears as a beardless young man reading a book by a window. The town of spires and chimneys is clearly labelled 'OXFORD'. Henry went to Oriel College, Oxford, in October, 1573, aged about sixteen. In those days students were admitted at a younger age than they are now, and so they were accompanied by a tutor to look after them and supervise their work.

Henry did not stay at Oxford long enough to take a degree.

This part of the picture shows Henry as a student at Oxford.

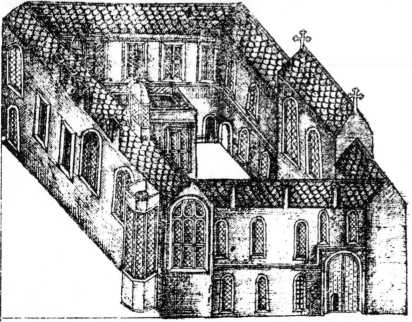

A sketch of Oriel College, Oxford, by a student who was there about the same time as Henry Unton. Compare this with the building in the life-story picture. That artist probably never saw the college. Notice the chapel, the hall with a louvre in the roof and the great oriel window.

Fathers of young men of Henry's position did not generally think this was necessary. Instead they preferred them to have a certain amount of legal knowledge, an essential requirement for anyone who owned land. Therefore Henry completed his formal education at the Middle Temple, one of the Inns of Court in London.

Still Sir Edward Unton did not consider that Henry's education was finished without a European tour. Such tours had become fashionable by the end of the century, but Sir Edward himself had made the trip before it was generally popular. He hoped that the experience of the tour would help to prepare Henry for a court appointment. Above the scene at Oxford is a strip of water which flows across nearly half the picture. This represents the English Channel. The precipitous mountains are 'Y ALPES' and Henry is shown with two companions (one of whom is his tutor) riding in the Italian countryside near 'PADDVA' (Padua). Henry is holding an umbrella, an 'ingenious Italian invention' that protects the rider from the heat of the sun.

Although foreign travel was gradually becoming popular, it was not without its hazards, particularly in Italy. English Protestants were in danger of falling into the hands of the Inquisi-tion and, indeed, such a terrible misfortune happened to Henry's brother Edward, in 1582. The Inquisition was an organization dedicated to eliminating religious heresy, that is any deviation from the doctrines of the Roman Catholic Church. There were agents of the Inquisition all over Italy who had the power to arrest and imprison suspects for long periods before trial and to seize their property. However, though Rome could be dangerous, Venice and Padua were comparatively safe. Padua's ancient university was the only Italian university that allowed English Protestants to study there. Venice was famous for the quality of its musical studies. Henry became fluent in the Italian language which was important for his later career as an ambassador.

It is most likely that Henry also visited Paris. This city was renowned for its academies that taught the arts of horseman-ship, fencing and dancing. He doubtless became fluent in French too.

We do not know exactly when Henry returned home, but it was probably about 1578. He was now ready to help his father to look after the family estates at Wadley and to embark on his own career.

3 Home life in a great country house

Henry's father, Sir Edward Unton, owned a considerable amount of property mainly in Berkshire and Oxfordshire, and to a lesser extent in Buckinghamshire. In the sixteenth century a man's wealth and importance in the community was measured in land, and with the land came certain responsibilities and obligations as well as power. His marriage to the widowed Countess of Warwick brought him more land in Warwickshire, and into the orbit of the new court of Queen Elizabeth I. Sir Edward was knighted at her coronation in January 1559. In 1572 he became a member of parliament for Berkshire and two years later, in July 1574, the queen visited his house at Wadley, near Faringdon.

Such a visit was considered a great honour. Each summer the court vacated the London palaces and set out on a 'progress' to different parts of the country. Hundreds of horses and dozens of carriages and carts lumbered along the pitted roads of the English countryside to the delight of the local people and to the acute inconvenience of the royal officials. The amount of luggage that accompanied the queen was astonishing; even her four-poster bed had to be dismantled and re-assembled each night, since she would sleep in nothing else. Though her ministers dreaded the summer progress, Elizabeth loved it. It gave her the opportunity to see, and to be seen by, a larger number of her subjects than lived in the

Queen Elizabeth I in procession, painted by Robert Peake the Elder in the 1590s. We do not know exactly where this is taking place but the scene would have been much the same at any place she visited on a progress.

London area. As a contemporary writer explains further: 'When it pleases her in the summer season to recreate herself abroad, and view the estate of the country and hear the complaints of her poor commons injured by her unjust officers, or their substitutes, every nobleman's house is her palace where she continueth during pleasure and till she return again to one of her own . . .'

In the expectation of a visit, gentlemen sometimes extended their houses or even built new ones. It was an expensive and demanding business to accommodate the queen and her enormous household – from the grandest officials of the realm to the humblest servants. As we have seen, the queen expected to be royally entertained; banquets, pageants, the hunting of deer and similar out-door pursuits were laid on. No cost was spared because no one wanted to seem mean in the provision of entertainment for the queen. Lord Burghley built his house, Theobalds, especially with royal visits in mind and yet he grumbled that each one cost him £3,000. The Earl of Leicester, in keeping with his position and his pride, entertained the Queen for three weeks at Kenilworth in 1575.

On the other hand, Elizabeth's hosts took advantage of their hospitality. As the source of all official appointments, honours, trading concessions and other favours, it was useful having the queen under your roof. You could take the opportunity to petition her for yourself or for your relatives.

It is not clear whether the queen stayed overnight at Wadley. At all events, Sir Edward must have provided at least one sumptuous meal in the Great Chamber at Wadley and he presented her with a handsome jewel: 'one jewel of gold garnished with diamonds and rubies and five pearls pendant [hanging pearls], one bigger than the rest'. His son, Henry, still a university student, would have been present on this occasion, although no reference is made to it in the memorial picture.

Soon after Henry's return from his continental tour he entered the service of Sir Christopher Hatton, a royal favourite and vice-chamberlain to the queen. (In 1587 Hatton became the Lord Chancellor.) As his father's younger son, Henry had to make his own way in the world because he could not expect to inherit much land. The careers open to him as a gentleman's son were in the Church, as a professional soldier, or at court. Henry's whole education was geared towards a court appointment, and his service with Hatton was the first

move in that direction. He was probably a kind of secretary or personal assistant to Hatton, who certainly thought highly of him. Another influential patron at court was Sir Francis Walsingham, the Secretary of State mainly responsible for the country's secret service. In 1580 Henry married Dorothy Wroughton who was a distant relative of Lady Walsingham. Like most marriages among the well-to-do, it was probably arranged by their fathers, but generally the young people's wishes were considered. Arranged or not, the marriage between Henry and Dorothy was happy.

In September 1582, Sir Edward Unton died after a lengthy and painful illness. The funeral was delayed for over two months to wait the return from abroad of the heir, Edward. He was a professional soldier in Italy, but on his way home to England he was seized by agents of the Inquisition and imprisoned in Milan. In the end the funeral had to take place without him.

To extricate him, Henry needed all the support he could get from the influential people he knew. With letters of introduction from the Earl of Leicester, Sir Christopher Hatton and Sir Francis Walsingham, Henry went to France and later to Italy

to negotiate his brother's release. For many months Henry tussled with the complexities of international diplomacy, aided by large sums in bribery. At last he was successful, his brother was released and returned home to Berkshire. It seems that imprisonment had undermined Edward's health; he deteriorated both mentally and physically. Though twice married, he had no heir, he was reckless with money and neglected his estates. He died in May 1589 on an unsuccessful voyage led by Sir Francis Drake and Sir John Norris to assist the pretender Don Antonio to capture the Portuguese throne from Philip II of Spain. So Henry inherited what remained of his father's land.

Wadley was one of several houses owned by the Untons. In 1596, after the death of Sir Henry, an inventory (detailed list) of his possessions was drawn up describing the contents of Wadley and Faringdon, his principal residences. This inventory is a very important document because it gives information about the extent of the household, the value of Henry's possessions and provides a typical example of what a man of his standing would have owned. The total contents of the two houses, excluding jewels and gold and silver plate, were val-

ued at £1,500. Elizabethan gentlemen had large households of living-in servants and entertained lavishly.

Wadley was a spacious house with several well-furnished rooms for entertaining guests and a large number of bedrooms (called chambers) for guests and servants. The compiler of the inventory describes, for example, the richness of the parlour (sitting-room). The furnishings included two tables, 'three green carpets, two green cloth chairs, one black wrought velvet chair laid with silver and gold lace, three long cushions of red satin laid with gold lace, thirteen green cloth stools, six field stools [folding stools] of leather, one cushion of Turkey work, and one other cushion, one pair of billows [bellows] and one pair of tongs . . .' The walls of each important room were panelled in oak and the ceiling decorated with moulded plaster. In some rooms the bareness of the walls was enlivened by tapestry, as in the Drawing Chamber (probably the grandest bedroom for honoured guests) and in Lady Unton's chamber. Elsewhere hangings of gilded leather were used, as in Sir Henry's study.

There were many service rooms in Wadley, some of which were in separate buildings. Besides the kitchen, there were dry

A woodcut picture of a country house. The house is surrounded by a moat which was unusual in the sixteenth century. A servant stands on guard by a drawbridge. In the garden behind the house two people sit in a bower. On the right a gentleman doffs his hat and greets a lady.

and wet larders, a pastry-house, a store-house, a bakehouse, a dairy, a brewery (ale being the most common drink in the sixteenth century), a cellar, a buttery, stables for horses, and barns for storing wheat, rye and malt. There was always a home farm attached to a large house for growing crops, vegetables, fruit and for grazing animals. A wealthy Elizabethan household was self-sufficient. Sir Henry had sixteen horses at Wadley in 1596, though one (we are told) was blind. There was also an armoury. Gentlemen of Sir Henry's position were responsible for equipping all the able-bodied men they employed. As there was no permanent army in Elizabethan England, everyone was expected to turn out and defend the country from attack, as happened in the summer of 1588. Once a year the Lord Lieutenant of each county summoned all men aged between 16 and 60 to present themselves for rudimentary training.

Such a large household needed careful management, and during Sir Henry's absences at court or abroad, Lady Dorothy and the steward (head servant) would take charge. Perhaps Sir Henry followed the example of his contemporary, John Harrington, who wrote down a set of rules for his servants, with a scale of fines for breaking them. Here are some: 'Item, that none toy with the maids, on pain of 4d; that none swear any oath, upon pain for every oath 1d; that no man make water within either of the courts [courtyards], upon pain of, every time it shall be proved, 1s: that meat be ready at eleven or before at dinner, and six or before at supper, on pain of 6d; that the court gate be shut each meal, and not opened during dinner and supper without just cause, on pain the porter to forfeit for every time 1d.'

The designer of our picture has given us a doll's-house view of Wadley, with particular scenes to illustrate aspects of Sir

Sir Henry in his study.

below: *Sir Henry and his friends playing viols.*

Henry's life and interests. Unfortunately it is not possible to identify with certainty the specific rooms we can see.

At the top of the house, Sir Henry sits in lonely splendour, probably in the panelled study hung with gilded leather and filled with two hundred and twenty books. Henry's enthusiasm for knowledge and encouragement of literary men is well documented by a number of prefaces written in his honour. He himself wrote a book, *De Legatione*, the duties and obligations of being an ambassador abroad.

Music was clearly important in the lives of Sir Henry and his family. In a small room on the left, a boy is singing to the accompaniment of a quartet of viols, which are different sizes of fiddle. The sheet music can be seen on the table. Three of the musicians, including Sir Henry on the right, wear hats, the mark of a gentleman. One of the most famous Elizabethan composers, John Dowland, published a piece of music for the lute, entitled 'Sir Henry Unton's Funeral'. A virginal, a popular keyboard instrument, is mentioned in the inventories of 1596.

Musical skill was considered a necessary accomplishment for an Elizabethan gentleman. Sir Henry probably played the lute and virginal as well as the bass-viol. His wife's relations the Walsinghams were a well-known musical family. Concerts at home, literally chamber music, became very popular. A group of instruments of the same family was called a consort: a consort of viols, a consort of recorders. If different types of instrument were played together it was called a broken consort. Just such a broken consort is depicted at the bottom of the detail above. The musicians, bare-headed, are professionals hired to accompany the dancers. The instruments they play are the flute, lute (plucked with the fingers and strung with gut), the cittern (plucked with the fingers and strung with fine metal), the bass-viol (played with a bow), the pandora (plucked and strung with metal) and the violin (played with a bow).

The predominant scene in the picture is the banquet. Sir Henry sits at the centre of the table, his wife, Lady Dorothy, is on the right. The particular occasion is not known, although judging by the entertainment, it must have been an important one. The room is most probably the Great Chamber, the largest reception room. The table is laid with a white linen cloth and, as everyone eats with their fingers and only sometimes with a spoon or fork, table napkins are draped over their shoulders or wrists. The most distinguished guests are seated on either side of Sir Henry.

Such a meal might take two or three hours to consume. There was a great profusion of dishes for each course, so that each guest could make a selection of what he liked. What was left over was given to the servants and anything still remaining was distributed to the poor. An Elizabethan gentleman kept up appearances by lavish hospitality.

In this scene, the feasting is over and the guests are watching a masque. Originally a courtly entertainment, a more simple form was performed in the private houses of the wealthy and became popular in the sixteenth century. In our picture, the earliest illustration of such an entertainment, the dancers wear costume, but there is no scenery.

The masquers enter the chamber in procession, led by a drummer and an interpreter. The interpreter has given an introductory speech explaining the theme of the masque, which he then presents to Lady Dorothy. Usually the masque theme was mythological, but topical references were included, especially compliments to the host and guests. The main characters in our masque are Mercury (with wings fastened to his costume to show he is the messenger of the gods) and Diana, goddess of the Moon and of hunting. She wears a sparkling headdress with a crescent moon and holds a bow and arrow. Diana is attended by six ladies, whose costume is similar to hers. They carry bows and bouquets of flowers. Also in attendance are ten Cupids, most probably children, walking in pairs. In each pair one child is dressed completely in black, the other in white. Long red and white streamers hang from their head-bands. They are holding torches, essential to all masques for they provided exciting light effects. All the performers wear masks on their faces to complete the disguise.

After the procession and presentation of the theme, the masquers performed a number of intricate dances. The entertainment was rounded off with the performers inviting the audience to join in the dancing. This was perfectly in order, because the masquers (unlike the musicians) were amateur performers of the same social standing as the guests.

Religion

The last room, the one with the tiled floor, is on the lower left-hand side of the house. Four gentlemen, none of whom looks like Sir Henry, are seated round the table. It is possible that they are a group of theologians having a religious discussion. Sir Henry was in contact with several religious scholars, one of whom, Robert Wright, was his chaplain in France and later became a bishop. This was an age when religion was a serious issue. Even within the major denominations – Catholic and Protestant – there was vigorous debate and furious rivalry among the different sects. Sir Henry was closely associated with the Protestant cause in both religion and politics, through his parents and his connections with the Dudleys, Walsinghams and Hattons.

A theological discussion.

Local government

When Sir Henry inherited his father's depleted estates from his brother in 1589, he painstakingly increased his fortunes by careful management. The rich furnishings at Wadley and Faringdon bear witness to that. He bought more land, including the manor of Faringdon, which he conveyed to Lady Dorothy for the remainder of her life. As a landowner of some importance and a holder of royal appointments, Sir Henry was an influential man in his neighbourhood. All local issues are likely to have involved him, and it is not surprising that he became a Justice of the Peace in 1592, a Deputy Lieutenant and a member of parliament for Berkshire in 1593.

Justices of the Peace, of which Sir Henry was one of about thirty in his county, were appointed by the Crown. Their responsibilities were far greater than they are today. They had to ensure law and order in the district and to enforce royal proclamations and parliamentary laws. Their duties affected the daily lives of ordinary people. For example, the justices

A woodcut showing an Elizabethan court scene. The magistrates and clerk sit at the table. In the foreground the plaintiffs are arguing their cause.

A felon is whipped through the streets and in the distance another is being hanged from a gibbet. From an Elizabethan woodcut.

20

were responsible for setting the annual wage rate for workers, based on the cost of living. The poor were their responsibility too. The justices ordered that those who were able-bodied but deliberately idle were to be whipped. To those who were too feeble to work they gave licences to beg. In a hundred different ways the central government relied on the co-operation of the justices. They received very little payment for their duties, but they accepted the heavy burden because they regarded it as the obligation of their class, and many of them doubtless liked to feel powerful and important.

Parliament

The practical power of parliament in the sixteenth century was far less than it is today. For one thing, parliament did not meet continuously as it does now. Moreover, it was the sovereign's privilege to summon parliament whenever (and only when) he of she wished. This was usually when extra money was required in time of war, or when the sovereign wanted a certain law passed. Sometimes years went by without parliament being summoned at all. The parliament of 1593, in which Sir Henry represented Berkshire, was summoned to vote for a large supply of money to equip the army. The House of Commons was unwilling to agree to the vote, because a large grant had been made only four years earlier in 1589. Instead, the Commons voted a grant of money that was the same amount as had been given in 1589. This was not enough for the queen. Influenced by Lord Burghley, the House of Lords voted for an increase of a third on the 1589 grant and put pressure on the Commons to accept it. The Commons resented this. Sir Henry was among several members who vehemently opposed the extra tax; he argued that the country was still suffering from the effects of the previous tax collection. In the end, the queen's ministers in the House of Lords got their way, but Elizabeth was furious with the MPs who had spoken in opposition to her wishes. As a result, Sir Henry was in disgrace for over three years and not received at court.

Queen Elizabeth I presides over parliament. In the foreground the Speaker, with officials and a group of MPs from the House of Commons, is addressing the queen who sits enthroned in the House of Lords. She is surrounded by her chief ministers and Lords of the Realm. The other members of the House of Lords sit in rows listening.

21

4 War

It is time to return to the picture. Above the line of water representing the English Channel, is a scene which takes place in the 'LOW COVNTRIES' (the Netherlands). Henry Unton is dressed in armour and two servants are holding his helmet and his horse. The town under siege is 'NJMINGGAM', presumably present-day Nijmegen in the Netherlands. In December 1585, Henry joined an army of 7,600 soldiers commanded by the Earl of Leicester, Countess Anne's brother-in-law. This army was sent by Queen Elizabeth to help the northern provinces of the Netherlands in their resistance to the domination of Spain.

In the map you will see that the Netherlands (which then included modern Belgium) was under the rule of King Philip II of Spain. After the upheavals of the Reformation earlier in the century, Europe had become divided into Catholic and Protestant states. Much of the history of Europe in the second half of the century is taken up with wars of religion. Sometimes a country was divided within itself and this caused civil war, as happened in France. In the Netherlands a number of people became Protestant, though most remained Catholic; but almost all resented Spanish domination, and after 1572 were in open rebellion against Philip II. The rebels took towns in

Sir Henry in the Netherlands.

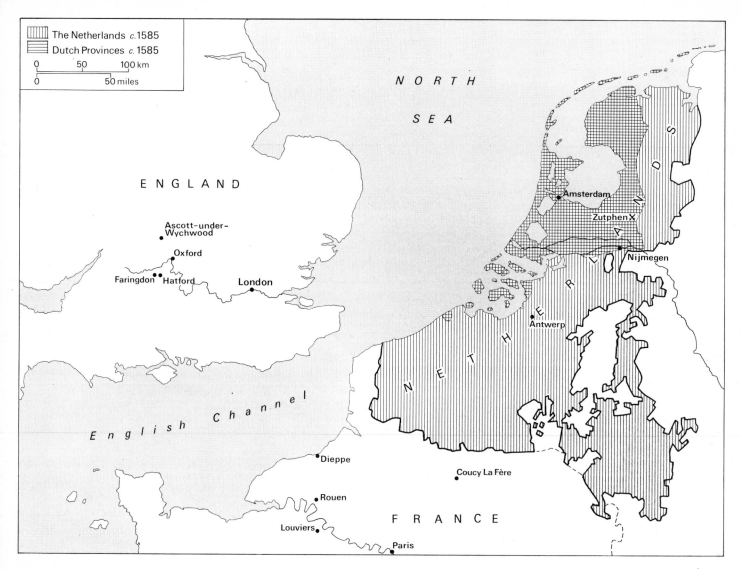

the northern provinces, and most Protestants joined them, but they were threatened by the Spanish army. For centuries the Netherlands had had close political and trading links with England. Now in their hour of need the rebels looked to England for assistance. England had been Protestant since the accession of Queen Elizabeth in 1558. However Queen Elizabeth was unwilling to provoke outright war with Spain, so she merely agreed to provide money.

Meanwhile the King of Spain was not idle. By the early 1580s the great Spanish general, the Duke of Parma, had regained complete control over the southern Netherlands and he was threatening the northern (Dutch) provinces, and Elizabeth feared that England might be next. The situation in the north became acute when the great Dutch leader the Prince of Orange was assassinated in 1584. Elizabeth decided reluctantly to take direct action. In August 1585 she signed a treaty with the Dutch provinces in which she agreed to send an English army to the Netherlands until the Spaniards were defeated.

Robert Dudley, Earl of Leicester, a favourite courtier of the queen, whom she had once been tempted to marry, was given command of this army. It was one of the few lapses in her judgement of a man's capability; Leicester was too inexperienced and arrogant to make a success of the expedition. At first he was enthusiastically received by the Dutch and he accepted (to the great annoyance of his queen) the title of Governor of the Netherlands. Unfortunately, his military activities of 1586 were a disaster and he quarrelled not only with the Dutch, but even with his own captains. In November he was recalled to England.

However, although Leicester's conduct in the Netherlands was a failure, his kinsman Henry Unton distinguished himself. The entire army was made up of volunteers, and Henry (as a gentleman) was probably a captain. Many sons of nobles and gentry flocked to volunteer for the opportunity of military glory. We can assume that Henry was a courageous soldier in the field, as he was among those knighted for bravery after the battle of Zutphen. Leicester commended him as an 'honest and rare gentleman ... who, with his companion, Sir William Hatton, hath not failed any journey since they came over hither, either on horseback or foot'. This suggests that Leicester employed Henry to carry letters and dispatches to and from his Dutch allies. William Hatton, Henry's closest friend, was also knighted at Zutphen.

The battle of Zutphen is perhaps best remembered now for the death of Sir Philip Sidney, the most admired Englishman of his generation. The tragic death at 32 of this distinguished soldier, diplomat and poet was mourned in February 1587 at a state funeral in St Paul's Cathedral. The occasion must have made a deep impression on Henry, for he and William Hatton were two of the knights honoured to walk in the solemn funeral procession.

We cannot explain satisfactorily why the town shown in the picture should be Nijmegen. This city was not captured by the Dutch until 1591 and Henry was certainly not present at that event. Although Henry himself took no further part in the wars in the Netherlands, it is important to note that the united northern provinces (Holland being the leading one) eventually won independence from Spain, though the southern provinces remained a possession of Philip II's descendants until the French Revolution. The division of the Netherlands and Belgium today is a direct result of the wars and religious disputes of the sixteenth century.

Robert Dudley, Earl of Leicester (1532–88), by an unknown artist painted about 1575. Notice his coat of arms with garter and earl's coronet.

5 Ambassador to France

Across the Channel we again see Sir Henry on horseback with a retinue of gentlemen. This time the countryside is France and the walled city is labelled 'CVSHIA', Coucy La Fère. In July 1591, Sir Henry was appointed English ambassador at the court of Henry IV, King of France.

This post was a responsible and delicate one. France was divided by a civil war. The Catholic party (called the Catholic League) refused to recognize Henry IV, a Protestant, as the lawful king. Henry was supported by the Protestants and some Catholics. The Catholic League was aided by Philip of Spain. As usual, Protestants in trouble hoped for English support. At first Elizabeth would send only money, but later she equipped two expeditionary forces, one of which was again led by a favourite courtier, this time the Earl of Essex. Essex was Leicester's stepson. He was handsome, popular, but rash. Sir Henry had got to know him during Leicester's campaign in the Netherlands and it was Essex's influence which gained him the post of ambassador.

This was an ideal appointment. Sir Henry had had considerable experience abroad, particularly during the tortuous negotiations for his brother Edward's release. He was also fluent in several languages. Sir Henry could reasonably hope that his success in the post would lead to more profitable appointments at court. No one made money from being an ambassador. The money allowance for food, transport, sending letters and intelligence services was never sufficient. Sir Henry had to pay out from his own pocket and hope that he would get it back afterwards.

He journeyed to France in summer 1591 with Essex's army. Unfortunately he became ill with jaundice as soon as he landed in Dieppe. The small inset picture uncomfortably close to the skeleton refers both to this illness and to the later fever from which he died in 1596. The huge four-poster bed is hung with red velvet and plumes of feathers. Sir Henry himself, wrapped in a nightshirt and cap is supported by pillows and

Sir Henry goes to France.

bolsters. A doctor kneeling beside the bed is taking his pulse. Others in the room are praying or silently thoughtful. There is a table of medicine bottles and bowls of lurid red liquid, probably Sir Henry's blood. A common method for reducing fever and (hopefully) the poisons of the disease was bleeding: a vein was opened and the patient's blood caught in a bowl. Another method was to apply leeches (blood-sucking worms) to the patient's skin.

The Elizabethans still believed in the medieval theory of 'humours'. Each person had four fluids or humours in his body; blood, phlegm, choler (yellow bile) and melancholy (black bile). A higher proportion of one of these humours determined the personality of the person as *sanguine* (good tempered), *phlegmatic* (placid, not easily excited), *choleric* (hot tempered) and *melancholy* (gloomy). We do not believe in the theory of humours today, but we still describe people with these words. Too much of any one of these humours could make the person ill and the cure lay in reducing or avoiding the wicked humour either with medicines or taking the patient's blood.

The queen was sorry to hear of Sir Henry's illness and wrote him a kind letter: 'Upon knowledge given us of your continuing sickness ... we found ourselves much grieved therewith that the same hath happened to you in a strange country, although we hope you shall be shortly recovered ... And so we end, wishing you to have care of your own health which we desire as much to hear of as any friend you have, excepting your own dear wife.'

Fortunately Sir Henry recovered. The hot-headed Earl of Essex soon got into deep trouble for ignoring the queen's command to stay in Dieppe. Elizabeth was anxious that Sir Henry should negotiate terms favourable to England before she risked her army in the field. Essex, and later Sir Henry too, rode off to visit the French king at Louviers and Elizabeth was furious with them both. As far as Sir Henry was concerned, the meeting was a great success, for the king was as impressed with him as Sir Henry was with the king. 'He is a most noble, brave king, of great patience and magnanimity; not ceremonious [but] affable, familiar and only followed for his true valour.'

The strategic city of Rouen was holding out against Henry IV. In October 1591 a joint force of French and English troops began a siege of the rebel city. For six months the Protestant armies surrounded Rouen. Then in April 1592 a Spanish army led by the Duke of Parma from the Netherlands set out to help her. So in June the siege had to be abandoned. Sir Henry was recalled to England, much to his relief because he was sorely out of pocket.

One event occurred in France which was remembered for a long time. The young Catholic Duke of Guise made an insulting remark against the queen in Sir Henry's presence. He felt honour-bound to defend her and challenged Guise to single combat. As it happened the duel did not take place. Perhaps the French king intervened, or maybe the Duke of Guise thought that Sir Henry Unton was not of sufficient importance to be worthy of such a duel. Sir Henry clearly had no such doubts, taking pride in his relationship with the Seymours, for he had written to Guise, 'nor would I have you think any inequality of person between us, I being issued from as great a race and noble house (every way) as yourself'.

Robert Devereux, 2nd earl of Essex (1566–1601) in garter robes. Painted by Marcus Gheeraerts the Younger, about 1597.

Soon after Sir Henry's return home, there followed the episode during the parliament of 1593, when he spoke out against the queen's tax. This led to his disgrace for over three years. Sir Henry now had few friends at court who would support his interests. The older generation, friends and relations of his parents, had died; the Earl of Leicester in 1588, Sir Francis Walsingham in 1590 and Sir Christopher Hatton in 1591. His most influential friend was now the mercurial Earl of Essex, who did his best to speak up for him.

Eventually in the autumn of 1595 the queen did forgive him. On Sir Henry's behalf, the Earl of Essex vigorously petitioned for the post of Treasurer of the Chamber. By December it was reported that the queen had agreed to the appointment after Sir Henry had returned from another mission. In other words, the profitable post of Treasurer would be his reward for a difficult (and expensive) tour of duty abroad. He was to go once more to France.

In 1593 Henry IV had changed his religion and become a Catholic. It seemed to him the only way to end the civil war in France. His conversion was a success, because the opposition to him in his own country soon collapsed. Nonetheless, the war against Spain continued and friendly relations with England were still necessary. The English haggled over the terms for their support: England wanted more advantages than Henry was prepared to pay as a price for assistance. Gradually the relationship between the two countries deteriorated and, furthermore, France and Spain were moving towards peace. If that happened, England would be left alone in the war against Spain – a very unpleasant prospect. It was to be Sir Henry's task to keep Henry IV friendly towards England and encourage him to continue fighting against Spain. But Henry IV had no intention of continuing an expensive war merely for the sake of England. The mission was almost impossible and not surprisingly Sir Henry was reluctant to go.

He arrived in France in December 1595 and rode immediately to Coucy La Fère (CVSHIA in the picture) where the French king was encamped. This time his reception was unpleasantly cool and he soon realized that he was wasting his time there, needlessly spending money. Soon his letters to the queen begged that she recall him, since he could do nothing to prevent a truce being signed between France and Spain. On 24 February he fell from his horse and, in a physically weak condition, he caught the deadly fever that had struck the French camp. Already one of his servants had died from it. When the king heard of Sir Henry's illness, he sent his own doctor to see him and even visited him himself. Sir Henry was most touched by his gesture of friendship and concern, and wrote: 'he [the king] had not feared the arquebus [gun] shot, and did not now apprehend [fear] the purples [sores on his body]'.

The king's doctor prescribed an extraordinary concoction. Sir Henry was given a medicine made of musk (a perfume), amber, gold and unicorn's horn. (Of course unicorns do not exist, and this last probably referred to the horn of the narwhal.) Furthermore, live pigeons were placed on the sore areas of his body in the belief that the fever would pass from the patient to the pigeons, and kill them instead. With cures like that, recovery was purely a matter of luck.

By late March, poor Sir Henry knew he was dying. On 20 March he wrote his last letter to the Lord Treasurer, Lord Burghley. 'My fever doth still continue with me, whereby my weakness is greatly increased. I have been again let blood and purged, but it doth yet nothing ease me: and so I most humbly take my leave.' Three days later, on 23 March 1596, Sir Henry Unton died. He was not yet forty.

6   The funeral

As he lay dying, Sir Henry remembered his friend, Sir Philip Sidney, who had died from wounds in the Netherlands. Sir Henry also wanted to be buried in England and it was his last request. Immediately below the death-bed scene, we can see the black sails of the ship carrying the body back to England. The castle on the sea-shore is possibly at Dover. The sombre procession with black-draped coach and horses winds its way to Wadley. A black crow, symbol of death, hovers above the trees. Beside the trees, villagers mourn the death of their landlord, who was honest in his dealings with tenants and servants, and generous with his donations to the poor. Above their heads are shields inscribed with words that are scarcely readable, which express their misery: 'This life grows worse and worse ... He is dead and gone ... Never greater grief ...' For the common people who worked on the land, or in the household of a gentleman or nobleman, the death of an employer or landlord would affect them directly. Would the new landlord increase the rents, or enclose more land and deprive the villagers of grazing rights for their animals? Would the household servants be re-employed by the new owner of the house?

As Sir Henry had died in office as ambassador, he was given the honour of a funeral service due to a baron, two grades higher than a knight. Such a privilege must have been a matter of great importance for the Untons, because the funeral is shown in such detail. The funerals of the wealthy were always grand affairs in the sixteenth century. The arrangements were made by officials of the College of Arms, officials called 'heralds'.

Sir Henry's funeral took place on 8 July 1596. The funeral procession led from Wadley to Faringdon church. Everyone in the picture wears black and the coffin is draped with black cloth on which is painted Sir Henry's coat of arms. The three heralds are distinguished by their brilliant tabards embroidered with the arms of Elizabeth I. The third herald carries a

Sir Henry's body is carried home from Dover to Wadley. At home the villagers mourn his death.

above: *The funeral procession to Faringdon church.*

left: *Faringdon church is packed with people listening to the funeral sermon. The scroll from the preacher's mouth cannot be properly deciphered.*

helmet with the griffin crest. One black figure carries a banner with Sir Henry's arms and two others hold pennons with his arms and the arms of St George, patron saint of England. The church is also hung with black cloth, and on this occasion it is crammed with people listening to the funeral sermon. The villagers who cannot get into the church clamber up the walls to see the procession.

It was customary for such a funeral to be followed by a large banquet. The left-overs were distributed to the servants and to the poor. We have no details of Sir Henry's funeral apart from the record of it made by the heralds for the College of Arms and a draft account of the costs which amounted to £27 16s 8d. This does not include the cost of the banquet. Perhaps the fact that Sir Henry was hugely in debt may have prevented the family from having a lavish feast.

Nonetheless, no money was spared on the enormous painted alabaster tomb installed in Faringdon church. It was the grandest of the Unton memorials there. Perhaps Lady Dorothy, who commissioned the tomb, paid for it from her own money. Alas the tomb no longer exists, and the picture probably shows a design for the monument which was not completed until 1606. The figure of Sir Henry, clad in armour, lies propped up on one elbow. Lady Dorothy herself is shown behind Sir Henry and the sculptured figures in the niches represent Faith (left) and Hope. Above Lady Dorothy's head are the figures of Victory (left) and Fame. The entire edifice is topped by two little cherubs with the figure of a griffin between them. The griffin, which you can see elsewhere in the picture, was Sir Henry's personal badge.

You can still visit Faringdon church and see some of the Unton tombs. Unfortunately the church was badly damaged in 1645, during the Civil War. While Faringdon House was under siege by the Parliamentarians, parts of the church were destroyed, including the spire and some of the tombs inside. All that survives of Sir Henry's memorial is the kneeling figure of Lady Dorothy, which was placed beside it after she died in 1634.

This was not quite the end of Sir Henry Unton. A group of his friends compiled a collection of Latin verses in his memory, which were published by the University of Oxford and called the *Funebria*. This honour had also been accorded to Sir Philip Sidney. But the most important and the most unusual memorial was the picture.

Sir Henry's personal debts amounted to £23,000 and he had left no will. This meant that the estate had to be sold in order to pay the debts and there were family squabbles over who would inherit Wadley and Faringdon. After many months it was settled. As Sir Henry had died childless, his brother-in-law, Valentine Knightley, the widower of his sister Anne, acquired Wadley on behalf of his three daughters. The house, which still exists, descended through the Knightley family. Cecily Unton, Sir Henry's other sister secured a claim on Faringdon after Lady Dorothy's death. Inventories of Wadley and Faringdon were drawn up and, as we have seen, both houses were well furnished and extremely comfortable by the standards of the day.

Despite his debts, Sir Henry had left his beloved wife well provided for. Her allowance and her right to Faringdon for the remainder of her life could not be touched. Wealthy widows were seldom left to live alone for long. Within months of her husband's death, Lady Dorothy was wooed by George Shirley, himself a widower. Lady Dorothy was too shrewd to lose her financial independence and a clause in the marriage settlement stated: 'if it should happen that she and her husband fall out, she requires £500 a year out of his living [income], and to live apart from him, with that added to her living of Faringdon'. It seems that she was never really con-

The brightly painted alabaster tomb with Sir Henry's figure clad in armour is typical of the period.

vinced that the marriage would be a success. Indeed two years after she married Shirley, she was separated from him and lived mostly at Faringdon until her death in 1634. She left precise instructions in her will that she should be buried quietly at Faringdon church alongside her first husband, Sir Henry Unton.

7 The memorial picture

In the months immediately following Sir Henry's death, Lady Dorothy comforted herself with the commission of the picture of his life-story. We do not know the name of the artist she chose. She carefully described to him the scenes to be included and the artist designed a scheme to fit the long rectangle of the wooden panel. We would expect to see Sir Henry's portrait given pride of place in the centre. The image is based on an earlier family portrait. It is typical of Elizabethan portraits to show a man's status and interests. His costume, like everyone's in the picture, is of the 1590s. Wherever he appears (and Lady Dorothy and Countess Anne too) he is proportionately larger than the other figures.

The sun shines on the happiness and successes of his life and the moon illuminates the scenes connected with his death. It is significant that nearly half the picture is taken up with dying and death. At a time when so many babies and children died, when to live until forty was considered a reasonable age, people had to think about death more than we do now. Memorials to the dead were very important and Lady Dorothy may have looked on the picture as a way of preparing herself for death, as well as a reminder of her happy life with Sir Henry.

It is unlikely that the artist ever went abroad. He probably made use of some contemporary prints, but on the whole he relied on his imagination. His painting style is old-fashioned compared with the court painters in London and particularly in Europe. He does not know the rules of perspective and the effect of the painting is rather like a medieval tapestry. But the purpose of the picture was not to create an outstanding work of art.

Lady Dorothy was able to enjoy her picture for over thirty years. She left the picture in her will to her niece, Lady Dering, whose christian name was Unton. Lady Dering left it to her son, but then we know nothing more about it until the early eighteenth century when it was sold to Algernon Seymour, later Duke of Somerset, a descendant of Sir Henry's grandfather, the first Duke of Somerset. He did not keep it for long. After several more owners it disappeared once more until the mid-nineteenth century. In 1847 it was discovered in an attic and sold once more. Its journey ended in 1884 when it was bought by the National Portrait Gallery.

You may wonder why the picture was so little appreciated in the eighteenth and nineteenth centuries that it kept 'disappearing'. This is partly because Elizabethan paintings were regarded as very old-fashioned compared with later styles and had little value. If Sir Henry had had children and his line had continued, then no doubt the picture would have remained in the family.

For us, though, the picture is an invaluable source for understanding the past. Sir Henry's career, his tastes, his possessions and his attitudes are typical of his age. Like his contemporaries we can admire his courage on the battlefield, and his determination both to rescue his brother and not to be brow-beaten by the queen's ministers in parliament. We can observe how he needed the help of influential friends and relations to advance his career; this was essential in Elizabethan England. Without them he could not have got so far, and had he not won their respect he would have remained an obscure country squire. Sir Henry Unton died some four hundred years ago and yet we are able to get very close to him through his letters, his inventories, the buildings associated with him, and particularly through his memorial picture.